Semi Colon ;

Leah Jones

Contents

Scars

Bruises. Bruises heal,

The scars will fade and peel.

Words. Words. Words.

They hurt.

When you drive that knife in such a way,

My confidence chips away.

Fat shaming and name-calling,

"Anxiety installing."

Too anxious to show my true skin,

Hiding behind L'Oréal and Maybelline.

Physical scars fade.

Emotional scars stay.

Self-love? What is that?

No one loves you when you're fat?

I can't be beautiful. I'm not told I am,

I'm on my own without that helping hand.

Emotions, hormones, mood swings,

I can't control everything.

A sledgehammer above my head,

Told to stay, told to go. I am the lead.

Want to hide, want to scream,

Want to take care of me.

Want to ignite the flame,

Not constantly take the blame.

Physical scars will fade,

Emotional scars are there to stay.

Headaches and a ruptured heart,

My emotions are a work of art.

I want to scream, cry,

I can't. I'm fine.

So desperately want to show what's inside,

Before my scars take over. Before I die.

The Fear

Fear. It manifests itself in you,

Builds a nest of tears and woe.

It's okay. It's only human,

To feel that sense of illusion.

You tell yourself it's nothing, you're fine,

But The Fear is shouting "you are mine!"

A knot in the pit of your stomach,

A force pulling you backward and forwards.

A paranormal wave of despair,

Hovering, leering, floating in the air.

Desperately holding on to a fairy-tale,

You try. But you fail.

Eventually, you succumb to reality,

Pulled by a force greater than gravity.

Ripples of worry in the river of sadness,

Gail's of anger in the hurricane of madness.

"It'll all be over soon"

Said the rain monsoon.

We've been here before and we'll come again,

Until you remember where it all began.

Visit us and overcome the fright,

Or we'll visit you at night.

In the dark, who knows what's lurking near,

Until you reach out and face The Fear.

I'll Try

I can't let them see me cry,

I'll tell them I'm fine.

I don't understand,

My tears? They're banned.

I used to dream in colour,

My eyes were filled with wonder.

Now? Now what?

Now I dream of anything but!

I made a promise to try,

But I still can't fly.

I can't see what you see,

It's so hard to believe.

Where do I go from here?

I've spent so long looking to the rear.

Forward seems so far away,

My dreams? Still grey.

I'll keep on trying,

At least I'm still surviving.

I brushed my hair today,

It's not much, well it is to me anyway.

I'm trying so hard not to fall,

Waiting for that one call.

I promise I'll try,

Even to just go outside.

Only if you promise me,

If I fail, leave me be.

There's a reason you won't see me cry,

I say I'm fine.

My bad days don't exist,

Will I even be missed?

Stupid. Stupid. Stupid.

Mustn't fall back. Stop it!

I'll keep my promise and try,

Maybe someday I'll fly.

Where Were You?

Oh, you're there alright,

When there's nothing to deny.

You were right there beside me,

When I was the best, I could be.

But where did you go?

I was the lowest of the low.

Where were you when I lay with an IVF?

Where were you when I was bereft?

Pan's Shadow that appears when there's light,

Then disappears in the dead of night.

I don't deny you're there,

But how much are you aware?

Did you notice the days where I never spoke?

Did you notice when I lay down and broke?

Would you have asked if I didn't say?

No. Not once did you ask? So, I didn't say.

You knew of my worries and woes,

And still, we only spoke of you.

You knew of my bereavements,

But we only spoke of your achievements.

You knew of my struggles and my strife's,

You never took an interest in my real life.

You pretended to. Very well,

Come to a disagreement, you like to dwell.

You ignore, insult, and you spite,

Until I come crawling back to the night.

Disrespect is a word you know not,

Denial is your favourite when caught.

Friendship doesn't mean much,

In a one-way street with a crutch.

Voiceless

The girl who always makes you laugh,

Cringes at the sight of her own photograph.

The one who calls you to check how you are,

For your well-being, she'll go far.

The girl you vent your feelings to,

Inside she thinks "best you never knew".

Though none is through lack of trying,

You ignored her while she was crying.

Did you know she cries herself to sleep?

She's taken that heart off her sleeve.

Where? Where is her phone call?

Just 10 minutes. That's all.

A voiceless echo in the canyon,

Desperately searching for a companion.

You may preach and think you know,

She's never seen anything so faux.

Again, she turns the other cheek,

She'll never speak.

Though she tries with small success,

Before it's shot back down. Compress.

She listens to your endless worries and tribulations,

Lord knows she's had her share across the nation.

She won't tell you half of hers,

For the sake of not being heard.

You may call her your saving grace,

But can you see the pain in her face?

She hides it well, though it plain to see,

She's dying for a hero like you and me.

She runs and walks for charity,

You say you're proud with little clarity.

She prays for vision and acceptance,

As she marches on for Mental Health Awareness.

Destruction

I don't know what to do,

I don't want to leave you.

Thoughts cloud my mind,

A disease waiting to unwind.

I sit staring into space,

Wondering about this place.

I stare into your eyes,

Trying to read your mind.

I stare at myself,

Don't reach for that shelf.

Destructive thoughts,

Leaves my stomach in knots.

Who will save me from this plague?

My pleas are not vague.

I don't know what to do,

I don't want to leave you.

A disease fills my mind,

Making me unravel and unwind.

A tight ship ready to sail,

Iceberg ahead. We've failed.

A cloud of deception and lies you are,

I begged. But you tore me apart.

I begged. I begged and I begged,

On my knees, I begged!

Ignored.

Swallow the sword.

Raise the broken shield,

Against the sword, try not to yield.

I don't know what to do,

I don't want to leave you.

I've had enough of my own mind,

Keep that shelf out of sight.

I'll try one more time,

I beg again but will you listen?

Or will the eulogies be your final lesson?

Is it enough I'm begging on my knees?

Or do you ignore everyone's pleas?

Silence Should Speak

Can you hear it? Listen.

Can you see what's missing?

We've not spoken in almost a week,

But if you listen, my silence should speak.

The room is still and quiet,

There's no sound. Not a single one. Silence.

Take a moment to look and really see,

Everything you're missing when you talk to me.

Mood swings, fatigue, and laziness,

Ignoring such potential greatness.

I'm tired, depressed, and weak,

If you listen, my silence should speak.

Though I've tried many times,

You're ignoring all the signs.

See the shadows under my eyes,

And be content when I say "I'm fine".

The more you look away and refuse to see,

My silence will not speak.

Conversations are dull and fading,

Listening to taunts and feel degraded.

I am grateful I'm not at my peak,

Listen closely, my silence should speak.

I have seen and experienced it first hand,

Bring me back down to safe land.

Feeling like an outsider. A freak,

Please listen. Or my silence will never speak.

Anxiety

Anxiety is a lot of things,
Most of all it's denying your feelings.
To be told they wish you were better,
Without the added pressure.
Anxiety is not leaving the house,
Stay inside where it's a safe little mouse.
Forever wondering if people are staring,
That's what I was told. You're comparing.
I wonder if people look at me and laugh,
Please, no photographs.
Anxiety is needing to wear makeup,
Make sure you put on that fake-up.
A constant need for reassurance,
Confirmation I'm not a deterrence.
Anxiety is knowing you're never enough,
Knees buckling, ready to give up.
To be told they wish you were thinner,
Everyone can see you, you're bigger.
To be told they wish they could brag,
I didn't think I'd done that bad.
Bragging rights of a size 6 and grade A's,
No. That will never be me.
On constant edge to pick up the phone,
Knowing a comment will come along.
They tell you it's for your own good,
But you wish they understood.
Anxiety is a lot of things,

That holds you down and clips your wings.

Anxiety gives you mood swings,

Never knowing what you're feeling.

To be told you shouldn't eat that,

Or your belly would be flat.

Anxiety is knowing you can't talk about it,

Staring at your nail, ready to bite it.

To be told your friends are pretty,

But you don't fit that committee.

Anxiety is a lot of different things,

I wonder if you get these feelings.

The Cabinet

Who's fault, is it?

The temptation of the cabinet?

At the time it seemed a good idea,

"You should lose some weight dear".

Words I should be used to,

At an all-time low, what could I do?

Words I've heard day to day,

Never knowing what to say.

Stress sets in,

Like a disease seeping into your skin.

Confidence? What's that like?

I imagine it's very dreamlike.

Self-conscious is my expertise,

No cure for this endless disease.

I ask again, who's fault, is it?

My hand slipped in the cabinet.

No one takes responsibility,

Not you, nor him or me.

My fault? Seems logical,

Your fault? Hysterical!

Why does there need to blame?

I guess there does in your little game.

No compassion or sympathy,

The anger is numbing as morphine.

I didn't mean to do it,

I was called to the cabinet.

I begged and cried for your hand,

You lied and said you understand.

Human resources were shameful,

I've never known such a betrayal.

A workforce of denial,

So-called advocates of suicide.

"Why didn't she come to us sooner?"

Oh, I did and the responses were fewer.

I sat in your office with tissue in hand,

Begging for someone to understand.

Shame. Shame on you. Shame on you all,

I did what I did and still, stand tall.

Who's fault, is it?

Maybe all of us pushed me to the cabinet.

She's Here

I see her there,

This fear I cannot bear.

She's watching me,

How did this come to be?

Countless sleepless nights,

Of bats, shadows, and heights.

With her pale skin,

I see her creeping in.

In my head and my mind,

Anger and fear intertwined.

Re-occurring dreams,

Of crying and deadly screams.

Escape this, I cannot,

She won't cease until I'm caught.

I try to run, try to flee,

I won't let her capture me.

The alarm clock sounds,

But to my dream, I am bound.

I awake with fright,

And wait for the re-occurring dream at night.

Dyslexia – For Dad and Joshua

Laughed at, cast aside,

Discriminated, patronized.

I find it difficult to read,

So don't alienate me.

I find it hard to spell,

I'm Dyslexic can't you tell?

Yes, I need extra time,

As words jumble before my eyes.

You say you understand,

And you'll lend a helping hand.

But truth be told you don't,

Because an exam is my warzone.

I battle and dodge the errors,

To hide from examination terrors.

You think you know, think you care,

Truth is, you just sit there and stare

At me as I read aloud,

When I'm done, I'm not proud.

I know inside you mock,

My confidence hits a block.

Don't judge me for the way I am,

Judge yourself for not lending me your hand.

My Nanna

You could have had anyone,

You could have left her alone.

Of everyone in the world,

My stomach churned.

Of billions and billions,

My heart broke into millions.

You had your pick of Evil,

Anyone bound to The Devil.

But you chose her,

You could have left us the way we were.

You stuck your claws in deep,

Waiting for her eternal sleep.

Cruel and wicked,

No sympathy. No pity.

Leave her to stay just a little while longer,

I will beg and scream for her.

Please don't take her away from me,

Leave. Just please leave her be.

I'm not ready. I can't lose her,

Please let me keep her, just a little while longer.

Hallelujah To You – For Nanna and Granddad

I'll stand here screaming Hallelujah,

I'll stand here in tribute to Ya.

I'll stand here staring at the stars,

I'll stand here wondering where you are.

I'll stand here remembering your smile,

I'll stand here smiling for a while.

I'll stand here screaming Hallelujah,

I'll stand here in tribute to Ya.

I'll stand here screaming "Why you?!"

I'll stand here denying the truth.

I'll stand here sighing to myself,

I'll stand here feeling sorry for myself.

I'll stand here staring at the hill,

I'll stand here silent and still.

I'll stand here screaming Hallelujah,

I'll stand here in tribute to Ya.

I'll stand here tearing up for you,

I'll stand here saluting you.

I'll stand here and turn around to go,

I'll turn around and walk on down.

I'll walk on singing Hallelujah,

I'll walk on in tribute to Ya.

I'll walk on humming Hallelujah,

I'll walk on in tribute to Ya.

I'll walk on remembering Hallelujah,

I'll walk on remembering my tribute to Ya.

Stress – Mental Health Awareness

Stress, it's a funny little thing,

It's never just a single feeling.

It's a knot in the pit of your stomach,

A gliding plane ready to plummet.

It's jealousy driving you mad,

It's creating memories you never had.

It's physical, emotional, and mental,

A writing pad without its pencil.

Imagine a Robin singing in the trees,

A song composed just for me.

Suddenly the singing stops,

You search every branch and rooftop.

Then you find that little bird who's lost his song,

Wondering where he belongs.

It's regret,

Finally understanding Romeo and Juliet.

Stress is denial,

Denying all thoughts have become suicidal.

Secrets and lies,

In the interest of loved ones, we deny.

Stress is heartache,

Knowing and accepting our inevitable fate.

A ticking timebomb of anxiety,

Never accepted in society.

Love and support, we think we have none,

In this world, we think we're alone.

Stress is a cult of warriors and survivors,

Some come home, some stay at war.

Marching uphill with "rifle and pack",

With one thing in common, "our plan of attack."

Who was I before the rain?

Someone in pain.

Who was I before the storm?

An actress, ready to perform.

I look up and see darkness,

I look around and see harshness.

I look ahead through washed eyes,

Thinking of all the lies.

Lies where I say "I'm fine,"

Close the door and I still won't cry.

For a while, I pretend and play the game,

But just like you, we're all the same.

Nowhere to run, nowhere to hide,

Nothing left so put it all behind.

Fight the demon within,

Be the victor and win!

No. The Demon stays,

At least for another day.

Hold it back and be strong,

Is what I try to do all along.

Be strong for everyone else,

I'm needed for everyone else.

My days are silent,

Like a ship taunted by The Siren.

Someday, I'll have my peace and in myself regain,

Whoever I was before The Rain.

My Worst Nightmare

Staring into space,

Searching desperately for my place.

A little bird lost in flight,

Not a nest or tree in sight.

My wings are clipped,

Slowly but surely losing my grip.

Staring at the medicine cabinet,

My unfortunate, intentional accident.

No foresight to what I'm doing,

I'm not sure what I'm pursuing.

One by one I start to take my life,

Yearning for that endless, dreamless night.

Panic! Panic! Panic!

Everything becomes automatic.

Blue flashing lights,

Trying and trying with all my might.

Surrounded by white walls of despair,

Sickness and disease everywhere.

With a needle in my arm, I sleep,

Wondering how I ever fell so deep.

Hear my pleas and remember,

Mental health is forever, not just a week in November.

Gatsby

A man of deception and mystery,

No one knows his real identity.

Parties full of sparkle and glitter,

An escape from the cold and the bitter.

Endless soirees of liquor and booze,

Countless meetings and rendezvous.

A personification of sophistication,

An idealistic fantasy of love and affection.

Nervousness, wealth and desperation,

Anxiety, self-loathing, and depression.

A true depiction of Prometheus,

Flying alongside the "great" Icarus.

An idiot Romantic with high hopes,

Taking you in and learning the ropes.

A perfectly charming "Old Sport",

On the end of his sleeve, he bears his heart.

Every generation needs a man of mystery,

Every girl needs a Great Gatsby.

Will I Be Your Muse?

When I look in the mirror,

I don't see glitz and glamour.

I see bags and dark circles,

Natural shades of blue and purple.

I don't see perfect cheekbones,

Or men lining up to be Mr Jones.

When I look at myself,

I see a girl ashamed of herself.

Ashamed of her body,

Ashamed of it all.

When I look at photographs,

I smile, I cry, I laugh.

I am not proud of my curves,

They send me wild, full of nerves.

I don't see sexy in the limelight,

I see dimples and cellulite.

I don't see cuteness or beauty,

I see a girl fulfilling her duty.

I see nothing special or exciting,

Nothing enticing or inviting.

"Should I compare thee to a summer's day?"

A fitting poem for how I feel every day.

When I look at my reflection,

I see nothing but imperfections.

I see crow's feet and freckles,

Patching hair and spectacles.

The more I ponder and think of it,

I will never be a must to your sonnet.

Talk?

Who can I talk to, really?

The answer? No one. Really.

You say I can,

But we both know I can't.

You say you're there for me,

But you ignore me.

Dark times come and go,

They fade, it's true.

But they never disappear,

Shadow's lurking are always near.

We try to pretend it's not there,

We try and pretend we're happier.

But the elephants in the room,

A mental illness' doom.

Talk? About what exactly?

A happier past me?

She doesn't exist anymore,

At least, not like you know her.

She fights demons and anger,

Rage and anxiety build inside her.

Help? Sure, she's asked,

It's always brushed past.

Here's a link to a charity,

Truth. Clarity.

Clarity her cries mean nothing,

To her, they're everything.

One fatal blow is all it takes,

To shake the building and its stakes.

A few crumbling bricks,

Not many. She still thinks.

Thinks of how she's judged,

Misunderstood and nudged.

Nudged into diets and insulting chatter,

I guess her feelings don't matter.

Anxiety builds. She won't go outside today,

She didn't go outside yesterday.

She won't leave the house on her own,

Surrounded by people and yet so alone.

Talk? Are you prepared to hear?

Listen you may, but open your ears.

Open your mind and hear her words,

Open your eyes and see her. Cursed.

Talk? To whom?

She tried once. Didn't work.

She knows she's alone. She's okay,

She'll be there for others, to live another day.

Nothing Prepares

How much can a person take?

How much pain? How much heartache?

How many more insults?

How many more ailments?

My eyes are dried, nothing left,

No time to cry. No time for much else.

Nothing explains the pain when you find it,

Hiding beneath the tissue and the fat.

My mind is reeling, stomach-churning,

Limb's ache, skin burning.

Nothing prepares you for that first lump,

In a gentle shower, you feel the bump.

Panic. Disbelief. Shame.

Stress. Heartache. Pain.

No words describe my heart right now,

Time for the final curtain call. Take a bow.

You've had your encore,

Please. No more.

You may not be what I think you may be,

You may be innocent until proven guilty.

In a jury of your peers; my medical staff,

Caught in a noose. Caught in a trap.

The mind still spins,

It could be anything.

Nothing prepares you for it,

You never think you'll find it.

I never thought I'd find one in me,

I thought I could be lucky.

Believe me, nothing discriminates,

In nature, nothing alienates.

We'll all fall victim to you soon,

Knee's buckle. Angel's swoon.

1 chance in 3,

To fall prey to the Big C.

Disconnected

What is this feeling?

Nothing and yet everything.

In silence, I sit and stare,

The walls grow bare.

I used to see sparkling stars,

Coloured diamonds in my bubble bath.

The colours have since faded,

I am Jaded.

I have day's where I feel nothing,

I have days where I feel everything.

I have days of woe and sorrow,

Days of no tomorrow.

No words comfort my heart,

Nothing short of a dart.

Never missing its target,

No. Don't. Stop it!

End these feelings of confusion,

Help me understand my emotions.

I am tormented,

Alone. Disconnected.

Wondering if I'll ever truly understand myself,

Does anyone understand themselves?

A lonely path I must take,

For that one smile I now fake.

Printed in Great Britain
by Amazon

86157994R10020